Brightest in the Sky

The Planet Venus

by Nancy Loewen

illustrated by Jeff Yesh

PICTURE WINDOW BOOKS
Minneapolis, Minnesota

Thanks to our advisers for their expertise, research, and advice:

Lynne Hillenbrand, Ph.D., Professor of Astronomy
California Institute of Technology

Terry Flaherty, Ph.D., Professor of English
Minnesota State University, Mankato

Editor: Jill Kalz
Designers: Amy Muehlenhardt and Melissa Kes
Page Production: Melissa Kes
Art Director: Nathan Gassman
Associate Managing Editor: Christianne Jones
The illustrations in this book were created digitally.

Picture Window Books
5115 Excelsior Boulevard
Suite 232
Minneapolis, MN 55416
877-845-8392
www.picturewindowbooks.com

All books published by Picture Window Books
are manufactured with paper containing at least
10 percent post-consumer waste.

Library of Congress Cataloging-in-Publication Data
Loewen, Nancy, 1964-
Brightest in the sky : the planet Venus / by Nancy Loewen ; illustrated by Jeff Yesh.
p. cm. — (Amazing science. Planets)
Includes index.
ISBN: 978-1-4048-3958-8 (library binding)
ISBN: 978-1-4048-3967-0 (paperback)
1. Venus (Planet)—Juvenile literature. I. Yesh, Jeff, 1971- ill. II. Title.
QB621.L64 2008
523.42—dc22   2007032874

Table of Contents

Star Light, Star Bright

It's early morning. The sun is rising. Look! See that bright star in the eastern sky? Long ago, people called it the morning star.

FUN FACT
Venus is one of the brightest objects in the sky. Only the sun and moon are brighter.

Now, it's months later. It's early evening. The sun is setting. Light fades. Look! See that bright star in the western sky? People once called it the evening star.

But these bright objects aren't two different stars. The morning star and the evening star are the same. And it isn't a star at all. It's a planet! The bright planet is Venus, named for the Roman goddess of love and beauty.

5

Earth's Twin?

Of our solar system's eight planets—Mercury, Venus, Earth, Mars, Jupiter, Saturn, Uranus, and Neptune—Venus is the second-closest to the sun. It's the closest planet to Earth and is similar to Earth in many ways, including size. Sometimes Venus is called Earth's twin or sister.

Jupiter

Uranus

Neptune

Saturn

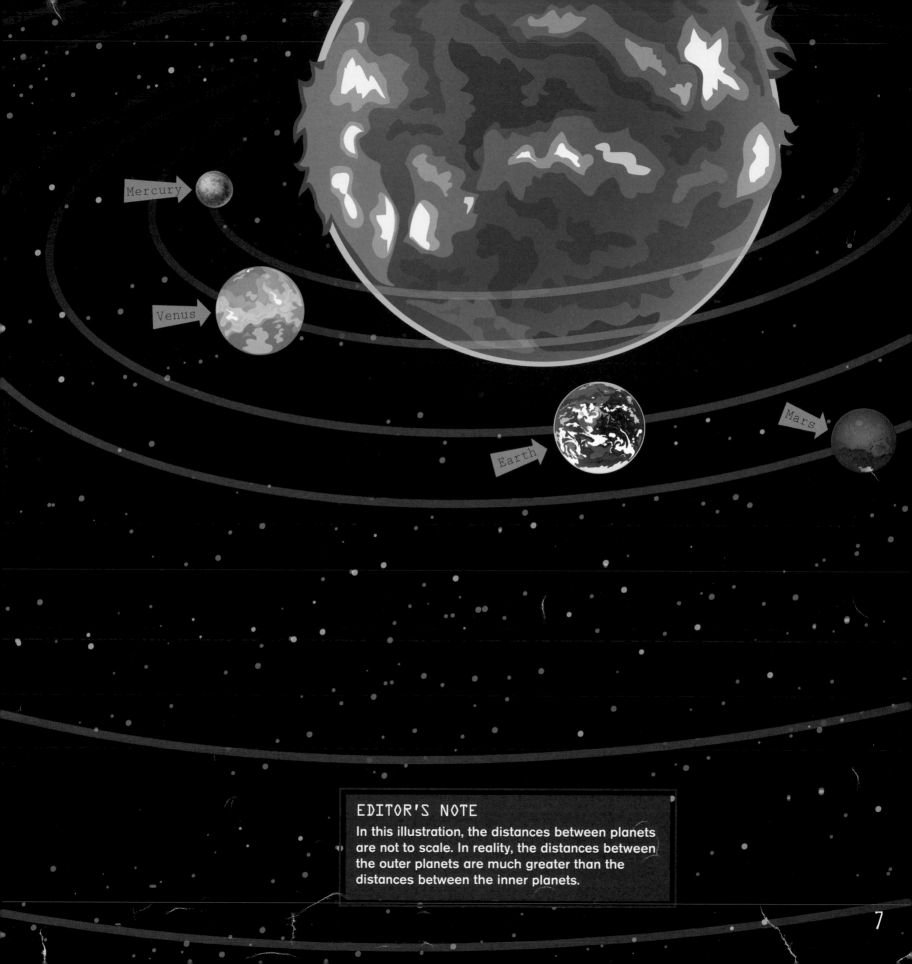

EDITOR'S NOTE
In this illustration, the distances between planets are not to scale. In reality, the distances between the outer planets are much greater than the distances between the inner planets.

Hot, Hot, Hot!

Because Venus is like Earth in many ways, people used to think there could be life on Venus. But scientists now know there is little chance that anything could live there.

The temperature on Venus' surface is about 870 degrees Fahrenheit (466 degrees Celsius). That's hot enough to melt metal! The atmospheric pressure is 90 times that of Earth. That's about the same as it would be more than half a mile (800 meters) beneath the surface of the ocean.

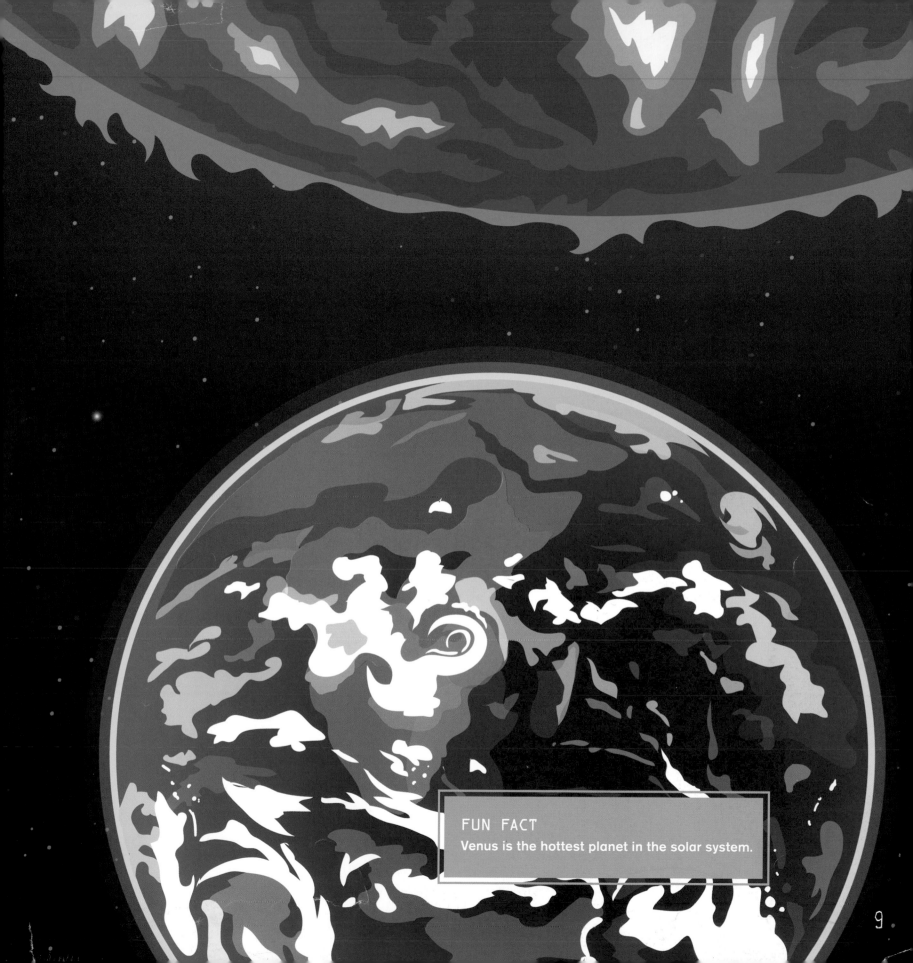

FUN FACT

Venus is the hottest planet in the solar system.

It's a Trap

Why is Venus so hot? After all, it's only a little closer to the sun than Earth is. And why is Venus hotter than Mercury, the closest planet to the sun?

A thick layer of gases is the reason for Venus' heat. This thick atmosphere doesn't allow much sunlight to get through. But when the sunlight does, its heat is trapped.

FUN FACT
Venus is very bright because it is covered with thick clouds that reflect sunlight.

Beneath the Atmosphere

At one time, oceans may have covered the surface of
Venus. But the water evaporated. Dry, flat land covers much
of the planet's surface today. There are also mountains,
valleys, and thousands of volcanoes, some of which may
still shoot lava into the air.

FUN FACT
Lava has formed some special features on Venus' surface.
Some "pancake domes," for example, are many miles wide
and more than 1 mile (1.6 kilometers) high.

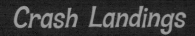

Crash Landings

Venus has around 1,000 impact craters. A crater is a bowl-shaped hole that is made by a hard object hitting the surface. Compared to Mercury and other neighbors in space, Venus has very few craters.

14

FUN FACT

Why don't small craters exist on Venus? Smaller objects burn up in Venus' atmosphere before they can reach the planet's surface. Only large objects can make their way through the atmosphere and to the surface.

A Long, Backward Day

Venus turns, or rotates, on its axis far more slowly than any other planet. A single day (one complete revolution) lasts 243 Earth days.

Earth

Venus is also one of the only two planets (Uranus is the other) to rotate in a clockwise direction, instead of counterclockwise. The sun rises in the west and sets in the east. The sun would never be visible from Venus' surface, however. The clouds around Venus never break apart.

Venus

Lying Low

To us on Earth, Venus never gets very high in the sky. The reason for this is that Venus is closer to the sun than Earth is. When Venus is moving toward Earth, it can be seen in the early evening. When Venus is moving away from Earth, it can be seen in the early morning.

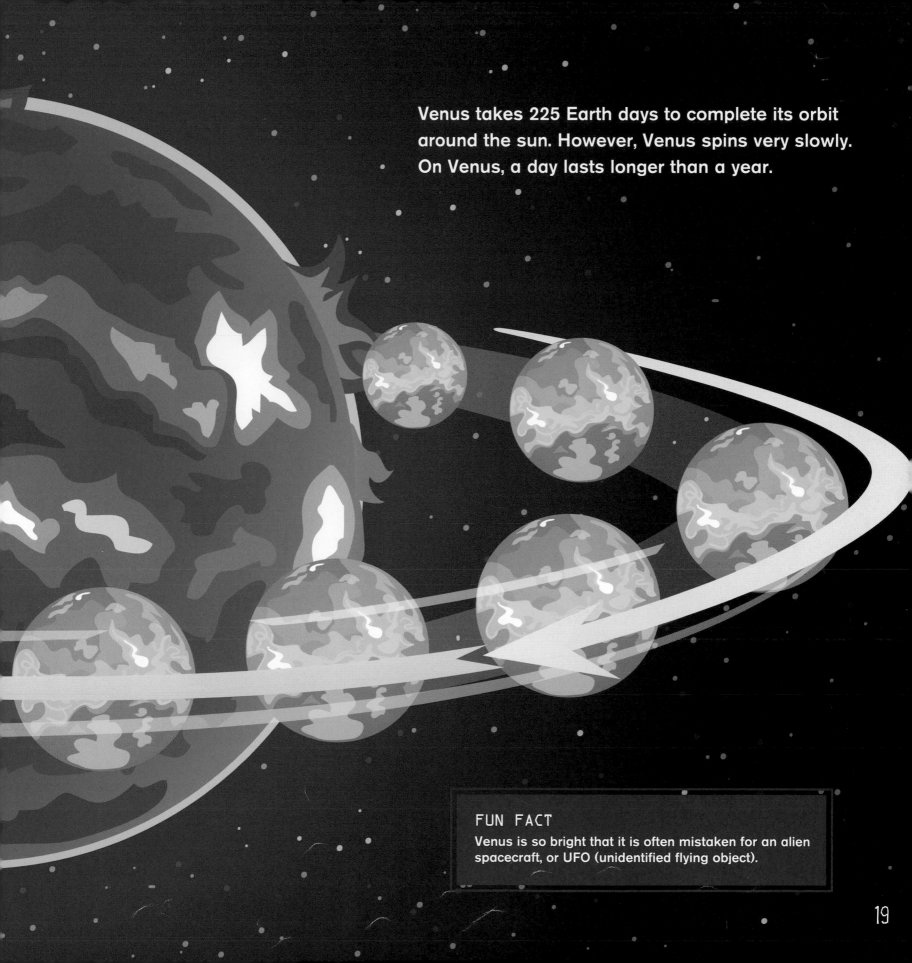

Venus takes 225 Earth days to complete its orbit around the sun. However, Venus spins very slowly. On Venus, a day lasts longer than a year.

FUN FACT
Venus is so bright that it is often mistaken for an alien spacecraft, or UFO (unidentified flying object).

Crossing the Sun

At times, Venus passes directly between Earth and the sun. This is called a "transit of Venus." Two transits occur eight years apart. Then, more than 100 years pass before the next pair of transits takes place.

The last transit of Venus took place in 2004. The next one will take place on June 6, 2012. Watch for it!

FUN FACT
Transits of Mercury and Venus are the only transits that can be seen from Earth.

Trapping Gases

- a jar with a tight-fitting lid
- a jar without a lid
- water
- a sunny place

What you do:

1. Put 1 teaspoon (5 milliliters) of water in each jar.

2. Put a lid on one of the jars.

3. Put both jars where they will be exposed to sunlight for a few hours.

4. After a few hours, check on the jars. Has the one without a lid changed? How about the one with the lid?

You'll probably see that the jar with the lid has steamed up a little. If you open the jar and put your face near the opening, you'll feel that the air in the jar is warmer than the air in the room. The heat from the sun turned the water into vapor (gas). But because the lid was on, the heat and vapor had nowhere to go. How is this like the atmosphere on Venus?

Fun Facts

- Venus has very little wind at its surface. Higher up, however, winds three times faster than hurricane winds push the clouds around the planet.

- In 1962, Venus became the first planet to be studied by a passing spacecraft, the *Mariner 2*. Since then, more than a dozen spacecraft have visited the planet.

- Venus has phases much like the moon. It looks full when it's on the opposite side of the sun. At other times, it's a crescent, or sliver. Its face is always changing.

- Venus' gravity is about 91 percent of Earth's. If you weigh 100 pounds (45 kilograms) on Earth, you would weigh 91 pounds (41 kg) on Venus.

Glossary

atmosphere—the gases that surround a planet

atmospheric pressure—the weight of the air above a surface

axis—the center on which something spins, or rotates

evaporate—to change from a solid to a gas

gravity—the force that pulls things down toward the surface of a planet

lava—molten (melted) rock that comes from inside a planet

orbit—to travel around a star or planet

revolution—to complete a circle around a central object

rotate—to turn on an axis, or center point

solar system—the sun and the bodies that orbit around it; these bodies include planets, dwarf planets, asteroids, and comets

To Learn More

More Books to Read

Asimov, Isaac, with revisions and updating by Richard Hantula. *Venus*.
   Milwaukee: Gareth Stevens Pub., 2002.
Rau, Dana Meachen. *Venus*. Minneapolis: Compass Point Books, 2002.
Simon, Charnan. *Venus*. Chanhassen, Minn.: Child's World, 2004.

On the Web

FactHound offers a safe, fun way to find Web sites related to topics in this book.
All of the sites on FactHound have been researched by our staff.

1. Visit *www.facthound.com*
2. Type in this special code: 1404839585
3. Click on the FETCH IT button.

Your trusty FactHound will fetch the best sites for you!

Index

Look for all of the books in the Amazing Science: Planets series:

Brightest in the Sky: The Planet Venus
Dwarf Planets: Pluto, Charon, Ceres, and Eris
Farthest from the Sun: The Planet Neptune
The Largest Planet: Jupiter
Nearest to the Sun: The Planet Mercury
Our Home Planet: Earth
Ringed Giant: The Planet Saturn
Seeing Red: The Planet Mars
The Sideways Planet: Uranus